JONAH TAYLOR

"He who fails to prepare, prepares to fail"

~ Benjamin Franklin

TABLE OF CONTENT

GENERAL PERMIT TEST –
90 General Questions with Explanations

TRAFFIC SIGN
65 QUESTIONS and Explanatory Answers

DRUGS AND ALCOHOL QUESTIONS
40 PRACTICE QUESTIONS

ROAD SIGN QUESTIONS
70 QUESTIONS WITH ANSWERS AND EXPLANATIONS

DEFENSIVE DRIVING
50 QUESTIONS WITH EXPLANATORY ANSWERS

ABOUT THE 2018 STUDY GUIDE

HOW TO PASS THE DMV PERMIT TEST ON FIRST TRY

NEW VIRGINIA 2018 DRIVING LAWS
Effective January 1, 2018

GENERAL PERMIT TEST –

90 General Questions with Explanations

1. If your turn signals fail, you should use _____ to indicate you are turning.
   A. Your horn
   B. Your headlights
   C. Hand signals
   D. Your emergency flashers

ANSWER C

Signals may be given by hand-and-arm positions or by using the vehicle's signal lights. If bright sunlight makes the signal lights hard to see or your turning lights are malfunctioning, also use hand-and-arm signals.

2. What kinds of drugs, other than alcohol, can affect your driving ability
   A. An allergy medicine
   B. Marijuana
   C. A cold remedy
   D. All of these choices

ANSWER D

When you drink alcohol or take other drugs, safe driving is not possible. Not every impaired or intoxicated driver causes a traffic crash, but each one is dangerous, putting the lives of himself or herself and those sharing the road at risk.

3. **Seat belts can be most effective as injury preventive devices when they are worn by**
   A. The person driving the car.
   B. Passengers when they are on a long drive.
   C. All occupants of a car being driven on an expressway.
   D. Passengers and the driver whenever they are in the car.

ANSWER D

Seat belts save lives and can prevent serious injuries in traffic crashes. This is why most states require seat belt use by adults in motor vehicles and seat belts, booster seats or child safety seats for children.

4. **To avoid accidents, drivers should communicate with each other by:**
   A. Signaling when changing lanes/direction, slowing down or stopping
   B. Using their horns in emergencies and when really necessary
   C. Using emergency flashers/flares/signs as needed
   D. All of the above

ANSWER D

Crashes often happen because one driver does something that another driver does not expect. To help avoid crashes, communicate with drivers on the road. Let others know where you are and what you plan to do by signaling your intentions with the help of your turn signals, emergency flashers, brake lights and your horn.

5. **A green arrow showing at the same time as the red traffic light means:**
   A. Vehicles going in the direction shown by the arrow must stop
   B. Do not go in the direction of the arrow until the traffic light turns green
   C. You may go in the direction of the arrow with caution
   D. Road closed ahead, go in the direction of the arrow

ANSWER C

A green arrow, pointing right or left, means you may make a turn in the direction of the arrow. If the red light is illuminated at the same time, you must be in the proper lane for such a turn and you must yield the right-of-way to vehicles and pedestrians clearing the intersection.

6. **When parking your vehicle facing uphill with a curb, you should point your front wheels:**
   A. Into the curb
   B. Away from the curb
   C. Either into or away from the curb
   D. Straight ahead

ANSWER B

7. **When passing a bicyclist, you should**

A. Blast your horn to alert the bicyclist
B. Move as far left as possible
C. Remain in the center of the lane
D. Put on your four-way flashers

ANSWER B

Move left to pass the cyclist, leaving a sufficient amount of space for safety. If there is oncoming traffic, slow down and let vehicles traveling in the opposite direction pass before passing the cyclist.

8. **What does it mean when a school bus is stopped and its red lights are flashing**
   A. You may pass if no children are on the road.
   B. You may not pass while the red lights are flashing.
   C. You may pass if you are facing the front of the bus.
   D. You may not pass if it is on the other side of a divided highway.

ANSWER B

Flashing red lights on a school bus means the bus is currently unloading children and they may be crossing the street. You have to stop and remain stopped until the lights stop flashing.

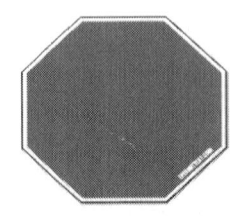

9. **When you see this sign, you must**
   A. Stop completely, check for pedestrians, and cross traffic
   B. Slow down without coming to a complete stop
   C. Stop completely and wait for a green light
   D. Slow down and check for traffic

ANSWER A

STOP SIGN. The STOP sign is the only eight-sided or octagon-shaped sign you see on the highway. At an intersection with a STOP sign, you MUST stop and wait for pedestrians and cross traffic to clear the intersection before you go again. Slowing down without coming to a full stop is illegal.

10. **After a train has passed, you should**
   A. Wait for a green light
   B. Proceed across the tracks
   C. Blow horn and proceed
   D. Check again for approaching trains and proceed with caution

ANSWER D

If you are stopped at a railroad crossing with more than one track, do not start as soon as the train passes. Wait until you have a clear view down both tracks before you start across. Even with one (1) track, do not start across immediately after a train passes - check again for another train that may be approaching.

11. You can drive in a carpool lane if
   A. You have the minimum number of passengers shown on the sign
   B. You are driving an empty 15-passenger van
   C. You want to pass the vehicle ahead
   D. You are in a rush

ANSWER A

An HOV lane is a special lane used only for carpools, buses, motorcycles, or decaled low-emission vehicles. You may use a carpool/HOV lane or on-ramp if your vehicle carries the posted minimum number of people required for the carpool lane, or you drive a low-emission vehicle displaying a special DMV issued decal.

12. What does the broken yellow center line on a raod means?
   A. You are in a no passing zone
   B. Passing on the left with due care is allowed
   C. Reduce your speed ahead
   D. No turns are allowed

ANSWER B

Yellow center lines located on a road means you should stick to the right of the line, unless you are overtaking a vehicle in front of you. When you are crossing the yellow line, it should be temporal.

13. **A broken white center line on the roadway means**
    A. No turns are allowed
    B. Reduce your speed ahead
    C. You are in a no passing zone
    D. You may change lanes with due care

ANSWER D

A broken white line separates two lanes traveling in the same direction. Once you have signaled and if it is safe to do so, you may cross this line when changing lanes.

14. **A rectangular-shaped sign is**
    A. School crossing sign
    B. Railroad crossing sign
    C. Stop sign
    D. Speed limit sign

ANSWER D

15. **A drivers who eat and drink while driving**
    A. Have no driving errors
    B. Have trouble driving slow
    C. Are better drivers because they are not hungry
    D. Have trouble controlling their vehicles

ANSWER D

16. This sign above means?
    A. No U-Turn
    B. No left turn
    C. No right turn
    D. No turning

ANSWER C

The sign signals you not to make a right turn at the intersection mark.

17. One of the rules of defensive driving is
    A. Look straight ahead as you drive
    B. Stay alert and keep your eyes moving.
    C. Expect that other drivers will make up for your errors.
    D. Be confident that you can avoid danger at the last minute.

ANSWER B

Traffic conditions change continuously. Always scan the road ahead. Do not use the road or even the vehicle ahead as your only points of focus. Look ahead so you can prevent, or decrease, possible problems. Keep your eyes moving, notice what is happening at the sides of the road, and check behind you through your mirrors every few seconds.

18. From top to bottom, the following is the proper order for traffic lights
   A. Red, yellow, green
   B. Red, green, yellow
   C. Green, red, yellow
   D. Green, yellow, red

ANSWER A

Red light is always located at the top if the traffic light is vertical and on the left if the traffic light is horizontal.

19. IF YOU DRIVE AFTER DRINKING, YOU SHOULD BE AWARE THAT THE FIRST THING ALCOHOL AFFECTS IS:
   A. Your hearing
   B. Your alertness
   C. Your vision
   D. Your judgment

ANSWER D

Alcohol affects those areas of your brain that control judgment and skill and is one reason why drinking alcohol is so dangerous; it affects your judgment. A person's judgment is the first thing affected after drinking an alcoholic beverage.

20. YOU ARE GOING TO MAKE A LEFT TURN FROM A DEDICATED LEFT-TURN LANE WHEN A YELLOW ARROW APPEARS FOR YOUR LANE. YOU SHOULD:
   A. Speed up to get through the intersection
   B. Stop and not turn under any circumstances
   C. Be prepared to obey the next signal that appears
   D. Go through the intersection since you have the right-of-way

ANSWER C

A yellow arrow means the "protected" turning time period is ending. Be prepared to obey the next signal, which could be the green or red light or the red arrow.

21. THIS WHITE SIGN MEANS:
   A. Drive to the right
   B. Right turn Yield
   C. Slower traffic should move to the right
   D. You must turn right at next intersection

ANSWER A

22. A TRAFFIC LIGHT IS RED, BUT A POLICE OFFICER IS TELLING YOU TO GO AHEAD ANYWAY. WHAT SHOULD YOU DO?

A. Wait for the green light
B. Change lanes and drive slowly
C. Do as the officer tells you
D. Stop and wait for the officer to approach you

ANSWER C

If a traffic officer signals you to stop at a green light, for example, you must stop. If an officer signals you to drive through a red light or stop sign, you must do it. Among the persons authorized to direct traffic are police officers, fire police, highway work area flag persons and school crossing persons.

23. ON A TWO WAY HIGHWAY, YOU ARE ALLOWED TO DRIVE ON THE LEFT HALF OF THE ROADWAY WHEN

A. There is a double yellow center line
B. It is safe to pass, and passing is allowed
C. You are approaching a corner at which you intend to turn left
D. There is a solid line on your side of the center line

Answer B

On a two-lane way, you are just allowed to drive on the left half of the roadway when it is safe to pass and passing is allowed. If the road has more than four lanes with two-way traffic, you should drive in the right lanes except under the condition of overtaking and passing.

24. A BROKEN WHITE CENTER LINE ON THE ROADWAY MEANS:

A. No turns are allowed
B. Reduce your speed ahead
C. You are in a no passing zone
D. You may change lanes with due care

Answer D

A broken white line separates two lanes traveling in the same direction. Once you have signaled and if it is safe to do so, you may cross this line when changing lanes.

25. You have the right-of-way when you are
A. Entering a traffic circle
B. Backing out of a driveway
C. Leaving a parking space
D. Already in a traffic circle

ANSWER D

26. THIS SIGN ABOVE MEANS
   A. Bicycle rentals are available here
   B. Children at play
   C. Bikeway crosses roadway, watch for bicycles
   D. Park entrance ahead, watch for cars

Answer C

27. THIS SIGN ABOVE MEANS:
A. Crossroad
B. First aid station
C. Church
D. Railroad crossing

   Answer A

It means a CROSSROAD. It is the intersection traffic sign.

28. WHEN YOU TOW ANOTHER VEHICLE, THE DRAWBAR BETWEEN THE VEHICLES MUST NOT BE LONGER THAN
   A. 5 feet
   B. 10 feet
   C. 12 feet

D. 15 feet

Answer D

The connection drawbar mustn't be more than 15 feet unless you are towing pipes, machineries or equipment that cannot be taken apart easily.

29. THIS ROAD SIGN ABOVE MEANS:
A. Stop if traffic is approaching
B. Three-way intersection
C. Crossroad
D. Railroad crossing

Answer D

The above signifies a Railroad crossing, and it is only positioned where tracks cross roads.

30. WHEN APPROACHING A BICYCLIST FROM THE REAR YOU SHOULD SLOW DOWN AND:
A. Wait until it is safe to pass the bicyclist with at least three feet of clearance
B. Tap your horn to warn the bicyclist
C. Follow at least five feet behind the cyclist till it is safe to pass

D. Stay as far as possible in the right lane without hitting the cyclist

Answer A

31. THE SIGN ABOVE MEANS:

A. A Sharp turn to the right
B. Double curve, right then left
C. Double curve, left then right
D. Pavement ends

Answer B

It means a SET OF CURVES from right to left.

32. THE SIGN ABOVE MEANS:
A. Low place in the road
B. Soft shoulders
C. Watch for pedestrians
D. Come to a complete stop

ANSWER A

33. BEFORE MAKING A LEFT OR RIGHT TURN, YOU SHOULD SIGNAL FOR AT LEAST

A. 50 feet
B. 100 feet
C. 300 feet
D. 400 feet

ANSWER B

You should move into the proper lane and signal your turn for the last 100 feet. You may decide to either use the hand signals or mechanical signals.

34. WHENEVER A LOAD EXTENDS TO THE REAR FOUR FEET OR MORE BEYOND THE BED OR BODY OF A VEHICLE AT NIGHT, THE END AND THE SIDE OF THE LOAD MUST BE MARKED BY:

A. Four red lamps and two red reflectors
B. Four red flags and two red reflectors
C. Four white lamps and two white reflectors
D. Four white flags and two white reflectors

ANSWER B

The following markers are used at night or in a situation when you can't see clearly: two red lamps on the back of the load which should be seen from at least 500 feet to the rear. Two red reflectors on the rear, which should be seen from at least 100 and 600 feet when directly in front of a low beam headlight.

35. THE SIGN ABOVE MEANS:
   A. Turn at the next intersection
   B. Divided highway ends
   C. One-way street ahead
   D. Road closed ahead

   ANSWER B

   DIVIDED HIGHWAY ENDS.

36. BRAKES THAT AUTOMATICALLY STOP A TRAILER IF IT BREAKS AWAY FROM THE TOWING VEHICLE ARE REQUIRED ON ALL TRAILERS EQUAL TO OR EXCEEDING A WEIGHT OF

   A. 2,000 pounds
   B. 3,000 pounds
   C. 5,000 pounds
   D. 10,000 pounds

   ANSWER B

37. THE ABOVE SIGN MEANS:
A. Two-lane road ahead, watch for oncoming vehicles
B. Road narrows ahead, prepare to merge right
C. Traffic merges with your lane ahead
D. Divided highway ahead

ANSWER C

It is a MERGING TRAFFIC Sign. Merge signs appear on expressways just before expressway ramps. Drivers entering from the right must yield to traffic on the main route, and must make use of speed-change lanes to merge safely and smoothly with the main traffic flow.

38. A GREEN ARROW SHOWING AT THE SAME TIME AS THE RED TRAFFIC LIGHT MEANS:
A. Vehicles going in the direction shown by the arrow must stop
B. Do not go in the direction of the arrow until the traffic light turns green
C. You may go in the direction of the arrow with caution
D. Road closed ahead, go in the direction of the arrow

ANSWER C

39. THIS SIGN MEANS:
A. Slow down, children at play
B. Watch for pedestrians crossing the roadway

C. Pedestrians stay on sidewalk
D. Come to a complete stop ahead

ANSWER B

PEDESTRIAN CROSSING. You should watch out for people crossing the street. Remember to Slow down or stop if necessary. Remember that people crossing the street on the pedestrian crossing have the right-of-way.

40. IF YOU DRIVE AFTER DRINKING, YOU SHOULD BE AWARE THAT THE FIRST THING ALCOHOL AFFECTS IS:
A. Your hearing
B. Your alertness
C. Your vision
D. Your judgment

ANSWER D

A person's judgment is the first thing affected after drinking any form of alcoholic beverage.

41. WHEN APPROACHING ANOTHER VEHICLE FROM THE REAR AT NIGHT, YOU MUST DIM YOUR BRIGHT HEADLIGHTS WITHIN:
A. 100 feet of the other vehicle
B. 200 feet of the other vehicle
C. 300 feet of the other vehicle
D. 600 feet of the other vehicle

ANSWER C

When driving behind other vehicles, you should use low beams within 300 feet of the vehicle ahead.

42. THE SIGN ABOVE MEANS
A. A blasting zone
B. An intersection
C. A crosswalk
D. A railroad crossing

ANSWER D

It means a Railroad crossing. This warning sign is usually seen whenever you are approaching highway-rail intercession.

43. UNLESS OTHERWISE STATED, THE SPEED LIMIT FOR A PASSENGER CAR ON A TWO- LANE HIGHWAY IS:
A. 35 miles per hour
B. 45 miles per hour
C. 55 miles per hour
D. 65 miles per hour

ANSWER C

55 PH is the maximum speed limit in Virginia, and it is still in effect till date.

44. THIS SIGN ABOVE MEANS:

E. Crossroad
F. First aid station
G. Church
H. Railroad crossing

Answer A

It means a CROSSROAD. It is the intersection traffic sign.

45. WHEN YOU TOW ANOTHER VEHICLE, THE DRAWBAR BETWEEN THE VEHICLES MUST NOT BE LONGER THAN

E. 5 feet
F. 10 feet
G. 12 feet
H. 15 feet

Answer D

The connection drawbar mustn't be more than 15 feet unless you are towing pipes, machineries or equipment that cannot be taken apart easily.

46. THIS ROAD SIGN ABOVE MEANS:
   E. Stop if traffic is approaching
   F. Three-way intersection
   G. Crossroad
   H. Railroad crossing

   Answer D

   The above signifies a Railroad crossing, and it is only positioned where tracks cross roads.

47. WHEN APPROACHING A BICYCLIST FROM THE REAR YOU SHOULD SLOW DOWN AND:
   E. Wait until it is safe to pass the bicyclist with at least three feet of clearance
   F. Tap your horn to warn the bicyclist
   G. Follow at least five feet behind the cyclist till it is safe to pass
   H. Stay as far as possible in the right lane without hitting the cyclist

   Answer A

48. WHAT DOES THE BROKEN YELLOW CENTER LINE ON A RAOD MEANS?

    E. You are in a no passing zone
    F. Passing on the left with due care is allowed
    G. Reduce your speed ahead
    H. No turns are allowed

ANSWER B

Yellow center lines located on a road means you should stick to the right of the line, unless you are overtaking a vehicle in front of you. When you are crossing the yellow line, it should be temporal.

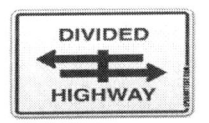

[DIVIDED HIGHWAY sign]

49. THE SIGN ABOVE MEANS?

    A. You must turn left or right
    B. You are approaching a T-intersection
    C. The road that you are on intersects with a divided highway
    D. Designates an overpass above a divided highway

ANSWER C

It means that the road on which you are currently driving intersects with a divided highway. It means you can only turn right at the first road, and left at the second.

50. THIS SIGN ABOVE MEANS?
  A. Entrance to full parking lots
  B. Entrance to road construction areas
  C. Entrance to dead-end streets
  D. Wrong-way entrance on one-way streets and expressway ramps

ANSWER D

51. IF A SCHOOL BUS STOPS TO UNLOAD CHILDREN ON A TWO-LANE HIGHWAY, VEHICLES TRAVELING IN THE OPPOSITE DIRECTION ARE:
  A. Not required to stop
  B. Required to signal, then proceed with caution
  C. Required to stop, then proceed with caution
  D. Required to stop until the stop signal on the bus is withdrawn

ANSWER D

All drivers going either direction of the school bus must remain stopped till the children are cleared off the road.

52. THIS SIGN ABOVE MEANS?
  E. No U-Turn
  F. No left turn

G. No right turn
H. No turning

ANSWER C

The sign signals you not to make a right turn at the intersection mark.

53. **BRAKES THAT AUTOMATICALLY STOP A TRAILER IF IT BREAKS AWAY FROM THE TOWING VEHICLE ARE REQUIRED ON ALL TRAILERS EQUAL TO OR EXCEEDING A WEIGHT OF**

   E. 2,000 pounds
   F. 3,000 pounds
   G. 5,000 pounds
   H. 10,000 pounds

   ANSWER B

54. **What would you do if you see this sign above your car lane**
   A. May stay in this lane and continue through the interchange
   B. Must exit the freeway if you stay in this lane
   C. May not exit the freeway in this lane

D. May continue through the interchange or exit the freeway in this lane

ANSWER B

55. A BROKEN WHITE CENTER LINE ON THE ROADWAY MEANS:

E. No turns are allowed
F. Reduce your speed ahead
G. You are in a no passing zone
H. You may change lanes with due care

Answer D

A broken white line separates two lanes traveling in the same direction. Once you have signaled and if it is safe to do so, you may cross this line when changing lanes.

56. THIS SIGN ABOVE MEANS?
A. Truck crossing
B. Road narrows, right lane ends
C. Divided highway ahead
D. Hill ahead

ANSWER B

When you see a sign like this, be prepared to change lanes or allow other cars merge into your own lane.

57. THIS SIGN ABOVE MEANS?
    A. All traffic must turn right
    B. Side road
    C. All traffic must go straight ahead
    D. No right turn

ANSWER B

This side road sign enters from the right. It is one of the warning intersections that alerts you on an intersection ahead.

58. WHEN PARKING YOUR VEHICLE FACING UPHILL WITH A CURB, YOU SHOULD POINT YOUR FRONT WHEELS:
    A. Into the curb
    B. Away from the curb
    C. Either into or away from the curb
    D. Straight ahead

ANSWER B

Point your front wheels away from the curb when parking your vehicle facing uphill. Don't forget to set the parking brake and place automatic gear shift in park. Shift manual gears to first. If these precautions fail and the vehicle starts rolling, the front wheels will hit the curb and stop the car.

59. IF YOU SEE RED REFLECTORS FACING YOU IN THE PAVEMENT EDGE LINE, THIS MEANS YOU ARE:
A. Approaching a stop sign
B. In a no-passing zone
C. Facing traffic the wrong way
D. Approaching a busy intersection

ANSWER C

If you see red reflectors facing you on the lane lines, you are on the wrong side of the road. Get into the proper lane immediately! Red reflectors always mean you are facing traffic the wrong way and could have a head-on collision.

60. BEFORE YOU REACH THE INTERSECTION, WHEN CROSSING RAILROAD TRACKS IN SLOW TRAFFIC, YOU SHOULD:
A. Sound your horn as you are crossing the tracks
B. Stop on the tracks until your light turns green
C. Stop between the crossing gates in case they close
D. Wait until you can completely cross the tracks before you proceed

ANSWER D

61. A DIAMOND-SHAPED SIGN IS A:
A. Road hazard sign.
B. Interstate route sign.
C. School crossing sign.
D. Speed limit sign.

ANSWER A

The shape of a diamond is reserved exclusively for warning drivers of existing or possible hazards on roadways and adjacent areas. Diamond-shaped signs are either warning signs or work zone traffic signs.

62. WHEN YOU HEAR THE SIREN OR SEE THE FLASHING RED LIGHT OF A CLOSELY APPROACHING EMERGENCY VEHICLE, AND YOU ARE NOT IN THE INTERSECTION, YOU SHOULD:
    A. Drive slowly in the right lane until it has passed
    B. Speed up so that you can stay ahead of it
    C. Drive to the right edge of the road and stop
    D. Choose any of the above options

ANSWER C

63. WHICH OF THESE STATEMENTS IS TRUE ABOUT DRIVING AND TAKING DRUGS?
    A. Only illegal drugs can impair your driving
    B. Even over-the-counter drugs can impair your driving
    C. Any prescription drug is safe to use if you don't feel drowsy
    D. All of the above

ANSWER B

64. WHAT SHOULD BE DONE IF YOU EXPERIENCE BRAKE FAILURE WHILE DRIVING?
    A. Look for an area to slow down and stop after downshifting
    B. Stop off the road and raise an alarm
    C. Keep pumping the brake pedal quickly
    D. Any of the above

ANSWER D

65. **WHEN THE ROAD IS MARKED WITH A SOLID YELLOW LINE AND A BROKEN YELLOW LINE ON YOUR SIDE YOU MAY PASS**
   A. Only in an emergency
   B. If you are on an expressway
   C. If traffic is clear
   D. Only at an intersection

   ANSWER C

66. **IF YOUR TIRES ARE NOT INFLATED TO THE PRESSURE RECOMMENDED BY THE MANUFACTURER, IT MAY CAUSE:**
   A. Low gas mileage
   B. Uneven tire wear
   C. Improper steering
   D. All of the above

   ANSWER D

67. **A RED AND WHITE TRIANGULAR SIGN AT AN INTERSECTION MEANS:**
   A. Slow down if an emergency vehicle is approaching
   B. Look both ways as you cross the intersection
   C. Always come to a full stop at the intersection
   D. Slow down and be prepared to stop if necessary

ANSWER D

68. WHO IS RESPONSIBLE FOR KNOWING HOW YOUR MEDICATIONS AFFECT YOUR DRIVING?
A. You
B. Your doctor
C. Your pharmacist
D. The DMV clerk

ANSWER A

69. WHEN YOU APPROACH A SHARP CURVE IN THE ROAD, YOU SHOULD:
A. **Start braking as soon as you enter the curve**
B. Start braking before you enter the curve
C. Accelerate into the curve and brake out of it
D. Accelerate through the whole curve to increase traction

ANSWER B

On curves, there is a strong outward pull on your vehicle, which is especially dangerous when the road is slippery. Slow down before you enter the curve; you do not know what may be ahead (stalled car, collision, etc.).

70. WHICH OF THE FOLLOWING IS TRUE ABOUT VEHICLES DISPLAYING A DIAMOND-SHAPED SIGN (INDICATING A HAZARDOUS LOAD)?
A. They are not allowed to drive on freeways
B. They are not allowed to exceed 35 mph
C. They must stop before crossing railroad tracks
D. They always have the right-of-way

ANSWER C

A diamond-shaped sign on a truck means that the load on the truck is potentially dangerous (gas, explosives, etc.). Police department and fire department officers know what to do if the load is accidentally spilled. Vehicles which display these signs are required to stop before crossing railroad tracks.

71. THE ROAD SURFACE IS MOST SLIPPERY:
   A. During a heavy rain or storm
   B. Just after the rain
   C. Just when it starts raining
   D. During a light rain

ANSWER C

72. WHEN YOU ENTER A FREEWAY, YOU SHOULD CHECK TRAFFIC BY USING:
   A. The inside and outside mirrors only
   B. Only your rearview mirrors
   C. All mirrors and turning your head
   D. Only your left side-view mirror

ANSWER C

73. TEENAGE DRIVERS ARE MORE LIKELY TO BE INVOLVED IN A CRASH WHEN:
   A. They are driving with their peer as a passenger
   B. They are driving with adult passengers
   C. They are driving with teenage passengers
   D. They are driving without any passengers

ANSWER C

74. YOU ARE WAITING AT A RED LIGHT TO TURN RIGHT, AND A PEDESTRIAN ON YOUR RIGHT IS

WAITING TO CROSS THE STREET YOU WANT TO ENTER. WHO HAS THE RIGHT-OF-WAY WHEN YOUR LIGHT TURNS GREEN?
A. The pedestrian has the right-of-way
B. You have the right-of-way only if the crosswalk is not marked
C. You have the right-of-way because your light is green
D. You have the right-of-way if you move first
ANSWER A

75. WHAT ARE THE COLORS OF A SIGN WHICH TELLS YOU THE DISTANCE TO THE NEXT EXIT OF A HIGHWAY?
A. Yellow with black letters.
B. Black with white letters.
C. Red with white letters.
D. Green with white letters.

ANSWER D

76. YOU MAY DRIVE ACROSS A SIDEWALK TO:
A. Avoid driving over a speed bump
B. Enter or exit a driveway or alley
C. Make a U-turn
D. Pass a traffic jam

ANSWER B

77. ON THE INTERSECTION, IF YOU SEE A GREEN ARROW POINTING TO THE LEFT, YOU CAN:
A. Go in any direction
B. Make a protected turn left
C. Make a turn left or go straight

D. Turn left only if there are no vehicles coming in the opposite direction

ANSWER B

78. **WHEN YOU DRIVE THROUGH AN AREA WHERE CHILDREN ARE PLAYING, YOU SHOULD EXPECT THEM:**
   A. To know when it is safe to cross
   B. To stop at the curb before crossing the street
   C. To run our in front of your without looking
   D. Not to cross unless they are with an adult

ANSWER C

79. **WHEN ROADS ARE SLIPPERY, YOU SHOULD:**
   A. Decrease the distance you look ahead of your vehicle
   B. Stop and test the traction of your tires while going up hills
   C. Avoid making fast turns and fast stops
   D. Refrain from driving at all costs

ANSWER C

80. **WHEN PARKING DOWNHILL AND THE CURB IS ABSENT, YOUR FRONT WHEELS MUST BE TURNED:**
   A. Towards the road
   B. Parallel to the road
   C. Towards the side of the road
   D. In the direction of traffic

ANSWER C

81. WHEN A TRAFFIC SIGNAL LIGHT IS NOT WORKING, YOU SHOULD:
    A. Stop only if other vehicles are present
    B. Slow down and stop if necessary
    C. Stop and then continue driving when it is safe
    D. Proceed through the intersection as usual

ANSWER C

82. IF A PEDESTRIAN IS IN A CROSSWALK IN THE MIDDLE OF A BLOCK:
    A. The pedestrian has the right-of-way
    B. The pedestrian must yield the right-of-way
    C. Vehicles have the right-of-way, but drivers must legally take care for the pedestrian safety
    D. Drivers must honk the horn approaching the crosswalk, to urge the pedestrian to cross faster

ANSWER A

83. WHEN MAY YOU LEGALLY DRIVE AROUND OR UNDER A RAILROAD CROSSING GATE?
    A. Under no circumstances
    B. When you can clearly see in both directions
    C. When the gate does not seem to be working correctly
    D. When you think you can drive through before it comes down

ANSWER A

84. WHENEVER A LOAD EXTENDS TO THE REAR FOUR FEET OR MORE BEYOND THE BED OR BODY OF A VEHICLE IN THE DAYTIME, THE END AND THE SIDE OF THE LOAD MUST BE MARKED BY:
A. White flags
B. Red flags
C. White lights
D. Red lights

ANSWER B

During the day, red flags help notify other drivers of danger. At night, it is safe to use red lights.

85. WHEN DO ROADWAYS BECOME SLIPPERY THE MOST?
A. After it has been raining for awhile
B. During a heavy downpour.
C. The first rain after a dry spell.

Answer C

86. FOLLOWING CLOSELY BEHIND ANOTHER VEHICLE:
A. Helps you avoid other drivers' blind spots
B. Is a common cause of rear-end accidents
C. Increases fuel efficiency
D. Is part of the standard driving test

ANSWER B

87. THE "THREE-SECOND RULE" APPLIES TO THE SPACE _____ OF YOUR VEHICLE.
A. to the sides
B. ahead
C. in back
D. all around

ANSWER B

88. IF YOU NEED TO SLOW DOWN OR STOP WHEN OTHER DRIVERS MAY NOT EXPECT IT, YOU SHOULD:
A. Use your emergency brake
B. Look over your shoulder for traffic in your blind spot
C. Quickly tap your brake pedal a few times
D. Get ready to blow your horn

ANSWER C

89. THE CAR BEHIND YOU BEGINS TO PASS YOU. YOU SHOULD
A. Maintain your speed so traffic will flow smoothly
B. Pull to the right and stop so he can pass
C. Slow down slightly and stay in your lane
D. Blow your horn to allow him to pass

ANSWER C

90. IF YOU SEE ORANGE CONSTRUCTION SIGNS AND CONES ON A FREEWAY, YOU MUST:
   A. Change lanes and maintain your current speed
   B. Be prepared for workers and equipment ahead
   C. Slow down because the lane ends ahead
   D. Speed up to avoid rubbernecking

ANSWER B

TRAFFIC SIGN

65 QUESTIONS and Explanatory Answers

1. **AT AN INTERSECTION OF TWO-WAY STREETS, AFTER COMING TO A FULL STOP AT A RED TRAFFIC LIGHT, A DRIVER MAY:**
   - A. Drive straight ahead if the way is clear
   - B. Turn left if the way is clear, unless otherwise posted
   - C. Turn right if the way is clear, unless otherwise posted
   - D. All of the above

ANSWER C

2. **WHICH OF THE FOLLOWING MUST YOU OBEY OVER THE OTHER THREE**
   - A. A steady red light
   - B. A policeman
   - C. A stop sign
   - D. A flashing red light

ANSWER B

Directions given by traffic officers take precedence over signs, signals or pavement markings. If a traffic officer signals you to stop at a green light, for example, you must stop. If an officer signals you to drive through a red light or stop sign, you must do it. Among the persons authorized to direct traffic are police officers, fire police, highway work area flag persons and school crossing persons.

3. **A GREEN ARROW POINTING TO THE LEFT ON A TRAFFIC LIGHT MEANS YOU MAY:**
   A. Turn left or continue going straight
   B. Turn in that direction only after you stop
   C. Make a protected turn in that direction
   D. Make a turn even if it may cause an accident, since you have the right-of-way

ANSWER C

A green arrow means "GO." You must turn in the direction the arrow is pointing after you yield to any vehicle, bicyclist, or pedestrian still in the intersection. The green arrow allows you to make a "protected" turn. Oncoming vehicles, bicyclists, and pedestrians are stopped by a red light as long as the green arrow is lighted.

4. **YOU ARE GOING TO MAKE A LEFT TURN FROM A DEDICATED LEFT-TURN LANE WHEN A YELLOW ARROW APPEARS FOR YOUR LANE. YOU SHOULD:**
   A. Speed up to get through the intersection

B. Stop and not turn under any circumstances
C. Be prepared to obey the next signal that appears
D. Go through the intersection since you have the right-of-way

ANSWER C

A yellow arrow means the "protected" turning time period is ending. Be prepared to obey the next signal, which could be the green or red light or the red arrow.

5. **IF THERE ARE STILL OTHER VEHICLES IN THE INTERSECTION WHEN YOUR RED LIGHT TURNS GREEN, YOU SHOULD:**
    A. Enter the intersection and wait for traffic to clear
    B. Move ahead only if you can go around the other vehicles safely
    C. Wait until the vehicles clear the intersection before entering
    D. Enter the intersection because you have the right-of-way

ANSWER C

6. **A STEADY YELLOW LIGHT AT AN INTERSECTION MEANS:**
    A. Go
    B. Yield to other cars

C. Slow down and prepare to stop
D. Stop

ANSWER C

7. **When driving on wet roads, you should:**
    A. Increase following distance to 5 or 6 seconds
    B. Decrease following distance to 2 seconds
    C. Not be concerned about following distance
    D. Maintain the 4-second following distance rule

    Answer A

8. **When driving on slippery roads, you should:**
    A. Use alternate routes
    B. Drive as you would on dry roads
    C. Increase your following distance
    D. Avoid crossing bridges or intersections

    Answer C

9. **You may cross a double, yellow line to pass another vehicle, if the yellow line next to:**

    A. The other side of the road is a solid line.

    B. Your side of the road is a broken line.

    C. The other side of the road is a broken line.

    Answer B

10. If an approaching train is near enough or going fast enough to be a danger, you must

    A. Slow down and proceed with caution.

    B. Not cross the tracks until the train has completely passed.

    C. Cross the tracks at your own risk.

    D. Find an alternative route across tracks.

    Answer B

    Answer D

11. If a traffic signal light is not working, you must:

    A. Stop, then proceed when safe.

    B. Stop before entering the intersection and let all other traffic go first.

    C. Slow down or stop, only if necessary.

    Answer A

12. What can you do to avoid the need to make emergency (or panic) stops while driving in traffic?

    A. Honk your horn to make others aware of your presence

    B. Look ahead and maintain a safe following distance

    C. Drive in the right lane only

D. Drive slower than the flow of traffic

Answer B

13. You are approaching a railroad crossing with no warning devices and are unable to see 400 feet down the tracks in one direction. The speed limit is:

   A. 15 mph

   B. 20 mph

   C. 25 mph

Answer A

14. Before passing another vehicle you should:

   A. Flash your headlights to alert the driver

   B. Turn on your four-way flashers to warn the driver

   C. Give the proper turn signal to show you are changing lanes

   D. Sound your horn to get the drivers attention

Answer C

15. Before passing another vehicle, you should signal:

   A. Just before changing lanes

   B. At any time

   C. After changing lanes

   D. Early enough so others know your plans

Answer D

16. With a Class C drivers license a person may drive:

   A. A 3-axle vehicle if the Gross Vehicle Weight is less than 6,000 pounds.

   B. Any 3-axle vehicle regardless of the weight.

   C. A vehicle pulling two trailers.

   Answer A

17. If you are involved in a traffic collision, you are required to complete and submit a written report (SR1) to the DMV:

   A. Only if you or the other driver is injured.

   B. If there is property damage in excess of $750 or if there are any injuries.

   C. Only if you are at fault.

   Answer B

18. When you tailgate other drivers (drive close to their rear bumper):

   A. You can frustrate the other drivers and make them angry.

   B. Your actions cannot result in a traffic citation.

   C. You help reduce traffic congestion.

   Answer A

19. A traffic light which has a green arrow and a red light means that

    A. You may only drive straight ahead.

    B. You may drive only in the direction of the green arrow.

    C. You must wait for a green light.

    D. Vehicles moving in any direction must stop.

    Answer B

20. The amount of space you need to cross traffic depends on the:

    A. Road and weather conditions and oncoming traffic

    B. Presence of a stop sign

    C. Use of your turn signals

    D. Cars behind you

    Answer A

21. What are the colors of a sign which tells you the distance to the next exit of a highway

    A. Yellow with black letters.

    B. Black with white letters.

    C. Red with white letters.

    D. Green with white letters.

Answer D

22. Drive below the posted speed limit when:

    A. Anything makes conditions less than perfect

    B. Others drive below the speed limit

    C. Entering a highway where there are other cars

    D. You are on a four lane road

    Answer A

23. The most effective thing you can do to reduce your risk of getting injured or killed in a traffic crash is:

    A. Wear your seat belt

    B. Limit your driving to week days

    C. Stay in the right lane on multi-lane highways

    D. Limit your driving to times between 3:00 p.m. and 6:00 p.m.

    Answer A

24. What is the appropriate action to take when approaching a railroad crossing that does not have signals (such as lights or crossing gates)

    A. Always bring the car to a complete stop.

    B. Slow down and be prepared to stop.

    C. Do nothing; all railroad crossings have signals.

    D. Increase speed to get across the tracks quickly.

Answer B

25. A solid white line on the right edge of the highway slants in towards your left. That shows that

    A. There is an intersection just ahead.

    B. You are approaching a construction area.

    C. You will be required to turn left just ahead.

    D. The road will get narrower.

    Answer D

26. When traveling below 40 miles per hour on a limited access highway, you should:

    A. Drive on the shoulder

    B. Use your high beams

    C. Sound your horn to warn others

    D. Use your four-way flashers

    Answer D

27. You may cross a double solid yellow line

    A. To pass a slow moving truck.

    B. To turn into a driveway.

    C. To pass a car if traffic permits.

    D. Under no conditions.

    Answer B

28. You may honk your horn when you:

    A. Have to stop quickly

    B. Are passing another car

    C. Have lost control of your car

    D. Are passing a bicyclist

    Answer A

29. You must obey instructions from school crossing guards:

    A. At all times.

    B. Only during school hours.

    C. Unless you do not see any children present.

    Answer A

30. Before turning, you should:

    A. Use your signal

    B. Turn the wheel

    C. Increase your speed

    D. Change lanes

    Answer A

31. If your turn signals fail, you should use _____ to indicate you are turning.

A. Your horn

B. Your headlights

C. Hand signals

D. Your emergency flashers

Answer C

32. Should you always drive slower than other traffic?

A. No, you can block traffic when you drive too slowly.

B. Yes, it is a good defensive driving technique.

C. Yes, it is always safer than driving faster than other traffic.

Answer A

33. As you near an intersection, the traffic light changes from green to yellow. Your best action would be to

A. Speed up to beat the red light.

B. Apply the brakes sharply to stop.

C. Be prepared to stop in the center of the intersection.

D. Be prepared to stop before the intersection.

Answer D

34. The safest precaution that you can take regarding the use of cellular phones and driving is:

A. Use hands-free devices so you can keep both hands on the steering wheel.

B. Keep your phone within easy reach so you won't need to take your eyes off the road.

C. Review the number before answering a call.

Answer A

35. You should honk your horn when you:

A. Are travelling through an intersection

B. Are passing a bicyclist

C. See a child who is about to run into the street

D. Are parallel parking

Answer C

36. When you park on the roadway, you should:

A. Use your four-way flashers

B. Park at an angle

C. Keep your turn signal on

D. Turn your lights on

Answer A

37. You just sold your vehicle. You must notify the DMV within ____ days.

A. 5

B. 10

C. 15

Answer B

38. Which of the following is used on some highways to direct drivers into the proper lanes for turning

A. Flashing red lights.

B. Flashing yellow lights.

C. White lines on the side of the road.

D. White arrows in the middle of the lanes.

Answer D

39. Your ability to stop is affected by:

A. Signal lights

B. Other cars on the road

C. The time of day

D. The condition of the road

Answer D

40. You are driving on a one-way street. You may turn left onto another one-way street only if:

A. A sign permits the turn.

B. Traffic on the street moves to the right.

C. Traffic on the street moves to the left.

Answer C

41. What vehicles must stop at all railroad crossings

A. Pick up trucks.

B. School buses and passenger buses carrying passengers.

C. Motorcycles.

D. Vehicles towing a trailer.

Answer B

42. You come to an intersection which has a flashing red light. You should

A. Come to a full stop, then go when safe to do so.

B. Stop only if cars are approaching the intersection.

C. Stop only if cars are already in the intersection.

D. Slow down and be prepared to stop if necessary.

Answer D

43. If an oncoming driver is heading toward you in your lane, you should:

A. Steer right, blow your horn, and accelerate

B. Steer left, blow your horn, and brake

C. Steer right, blow your horn, and brake

D. Stay in the center of your lane, blow your horn, and brake

Answer C

44. **WHEN YOU ARE IN A DEDICATED TURN LANE CONTROLLED BY A GREEN ARROW, WHICH OF THE FOLLOWING IS TRUE?**
    A. All vehicles or pedestrians in the intersection must yield to you
    B. All oncoming traffic is stopped by red lights
    C. You may turn in the direction the arrow is pointing without checking traffic
    D. All of the above

ANSWER B

45. **You may cross a single solid white line in the highway**

    A. Whenever you want to.

    B. If traffic conditions require.

    C. Only to turn into a driveway.

    D. Only to make a u-turn.

    Answer B

46. **What does a flashing yellow light mean**

    A. Merging traffic.

    B. Proceed with caution.

C. Pedestrian crossing.

D. Come to a full stop.

Answer B

47. **You are driving on a freeway posted for 65 MPH. The traffic is traveling at 70 MPH. You may legally drive:**

    A. 70 mph or faster to keep up with the speed of traffic.

    B. Between 65 mph and 70 mph.

    C. No faster than 65 mph.

    Answer C

48. **If traffic prevents you from crossing all the way across a set of railroad tracks, you may proceed only when**

    A. An approaching train is not moving fast enough to be a danger.

    B. There is room for your vehicle on the other side.

    C. At least one-half of your vehicle can cross the tracks.

    D. No trains are in sight.

    Answer B

49. **If you need to slow down or stop when other drivers may not expect it, you should:**

    A. Quickly tap your brake pedal a few times

B. Use your emergency brake

C. Look over your shoulder for traffic in your blind spot

D. Get ready to blow your horn

Answer A

50. **At highway speeds, on a dry road, a safe following distance is at least:**

A. 3 seconds of following distance from the car ahead of you

B. 2 seconds of following distance from the car ahead of you

C. 4 seconds of following distance from the car ahead of you

D. 2 car lengths of following distance from the car ahead of you

Answer C

51. **Your blind spot is the area of the road:**

A. You cannot see without moving your head

B. Directly behind your vehicle

C. You see in your rearview mirror

D. You see in your side mirror

Answer A

52. When driving on wet roads, you should:

    A. Drive the speed limit

    B. Drive slightly faster than the speed limit

    C. Drive 5 to 10 miles below the speed limit

    D. Stay close to the vehicle ahead

    Answer C

53. A diamond-shaped sign is a

    A. Road hazard sign.

    B. Interstate route sign.

    C. School crossing sign.

    D. Speed limit sign.

    Answer A

54. You see a signal person at a road construction site ahead. You should obey his or her instructions:

    A. Only if you see orange cones on the road ahead.

    B. Unless they conflict with existing signs, signals, or laws.

    C. At all times.

    Answer C

55. IT IS ILLEGAL TO ENTER AN INTERSECTION WHEN:

A. You cannot cross without obstructing traffic on either side
B. The lane you want to enter is blocked
C. The light is yellow
D. The light is flashing yellow and you have not come to a complete stop first

ANSWER A

56. YOU WANT TO TURN LEFT AT AN INTERSECTION. THE LIGHT IS GREEN BUT ONCOMING TRAFFIC IS HEAVY. YOU SHOULD
A. Use the next intersection
B. Wait at the crosswalk for traffic to clear
C. Wait in the center of the intersection for traffic to clear
D. Take the right-of-way since you have the light

ANSWER C

57. IF YOU ARE STOPPED AT AN INTERSECTION AND THE TRAFFIC LIGHT JUST TURNED GREEN, CAN YOU GO IMMEDIATELY?
A. Yes, you now have the right-of-way
B. Yes, but yield to any vehicle or person still in the intersection
C. Yes, other traffic or pedestrians must yield to you
D. Yes, if you are going straight through the intersection

ANSWER B

58. A GREEN ARROW SHOWING AT THE SAME TIME AS THE RED TRAFFIC LIGHT MEANS:

    A. Vehicles going in the direction shown by the arrow must stop
    B. Do not go in the direction of the arrow until the traffic light turns green
    C. You may go in the direction of the arrow with caution
    D. Road closed ahead, go in the direction of the arrow

ANSWER C

A green arrow, pointing right or left, means you may make a turn in the direction of the arrow. If the red light is illuminated at the same time, you must be in the proper lane for such a turn and you must yield the right-of-way to vehicles and pedestrians clearing the intersection.

59. WHAT IS THE APPROPRIATE ACTION TO TAKE WHEN APPROACHING A RAILROAD CROSSING THAT DOES NOT HAVE SIGNALS (SUCH AS LIGHTS OR CROSSING GATES)

    A. Always bring the car to a complete stop.
    B. Slow down and be prepared to stop.
    C. Do nothing; all railroad crossings have signals.
    D. Increase speed to get across the tracks quickly.

ANSWER B

60. WHEN A TRAFFIC SIGNAL LIGHT IS NOT WORKING, YOU SHOULD:

    A. Stop only if other vehicles are present
    B. Slow down and stop if necessary
    C. Stop and then continue driving when it is safe
    D. Proceed through the intersection as usual

ANSWER C

Whenever there is a traffic signal blackout, proceed cautiously as if the intersection is controlled by "STOP" signs in all directions.

DRUGS AND ALCOHOL QUESTIONS

40 PRACTICE QUESTIONS

1. _____ HAVE EFFECTS SIMILAR TO THOSE OF LSD, BUT WITH STRONGER EFFECTS OF DULLED SENSES, LOSS OF SENSE OF SELF, AND SEDATION.
   A. Antihistamines
   B. Barbiturates
   C. Dissociatives
   D. Opioids

ANSWER C

2. WHICH OF THE FOLLOWING IS A MOTOR VEHICLE ACCORDING TO VIRGINIA LAW?
   A. A bicycle
   B. A motorized bicycle
   C. A motorized wheelchair
   D. A school bus

ANSWER D

3. THE _____ BREAKS DOWN COMPLEX MOLECULES INTO SIMPLER PARTS AND ALLOWS THEM TO BE CARRIED OUT OF THE BODY AS WASTE.
   A. pancreas
   B. bladder
   C. liver
   D. none of the above

ANSWER C

4. THE EFFECT OF ALCOHOL ON THE HUMAN BODY IS TO _____.
   A. cause feelings of happiness
   B. cause feelings of pleasure
   C. slow down bodily functions until eventually they stop
   D. increase heart rate

ANSWER C

5. EFFECTS OF CHRONIC _____ USE INCLUDE EMPHYSEMA, HEART DISEASE, STROKE, IMPOTENCE, INFERTILITY, STRESS, AND CANCER OF NUMEROUS ORGANS.
   A. tobacco
   B. heroin
   C. cocaine
   D. alcohol

ANSWER A

6. ACUTE CAUSES OF ALCOHOL-RELATED DEATHS ARE LED BY TRAFFIC COLLISIONS, FOLLOWED BY _____.
   A. homicides and drug toxicity
   B. suicides and falls
   C. homicides and suicides
   D. falls and drug toxicity

ANSWER C

7. FOR WHAT REASON IS IT RECOMMENDED TO TILT YOUR STEERING WHEEL DOWNWARD, IF IT IS ADJUSTABLE?
   A. To point the air bag towards your chest instead of your head
   B. To create better leverage for steering
   C. To increase your distance from the air bag
   D. To remove it from your view of the road

ANSWER A

8. WHICH OF THE FOLLOWING BEST DESCRIBES WHO MUST ACCOMPANY THE LEARNER FOR LEGAL USE OF A LEARNERS LICENSE?
   A. A person with at least an Intermediate license
   B. A family member
   C. A licensed driver at least 21 years old in the front passenger seat
   D. A licensed driver at least 21 years old in any seat

ANSWER C

26. IF YOU PROVIDED FALSE INFORMATION IN YOUR DRIVERS LICENSE APPLICATION, YOUR LICENSE WILL BE _____.

   A. revoked
   B. suspended
   C. cancelled
   D. restricted

ANSWER C

9. WHEN DRINKING AT A PRIVATE EVENT, YOU SHOULD ASSUME THAT DRINKS WILL _____.

A. be stronger than normal
B. be weaker than normal
C. not consistently have the same strength
D. be made with unusual liquors

ANSWER C

10. IMPAIRED DRIVERS OFTEN _____ WITHOUT CHECKING FOR CROSS TRAFFIC OR PEDESTRIANS.

A. stare straight ahead
B. scan the road ahead
C. obey almost all traffic laws
D. None of the above

ANSWER A

11. IT IS ILLEGAL TO MODIFY YOUR _____ SYSTEM OR INSTALL A BYPASS DEVICE TO INCREASE THE NOISE LEVEL OF YOUR VEHICLE.

A. cooling
B. exhaust
C. evaporative emissions
D. None of the above

ANSWER B

12. WHEN THE LIVER AND KIDNEYS ARE OVERBURDENED BY CHRONIC ALCOHOL USE, THEY CAN INCREASE _____

A. the rate of metabolism of nutrients
B. the production of white blood cells
C. the amount of harmful substances released into the bloodstream
D. A and C

ANSWER C

13. THE PENALTIES FOR A FIRST-TIME DUI CHARGE INCLUDE REVOCATION OF DRIVERS LICENSE FOR _____.

A. 180 days
B. between 180 days and one year
C. between 90 and 180 days
D. one year

ANSWER B

14. INHALANTS INCLUDE CHEMICALS FOUND IN _____.

A. shampoo and conditioner
B. paint thinners, lighter fluid, and glue
C. whipped cream spray bottles
D. B and C

ANSWER D

15. WHAT IS THE MAXIMUM FINE PERMITTED FOR A FOURTH DUI CONVICTION?

A. 10000
B. 20000
C. 50000
D. There is no maximum fine for a fourth DUI conviction.

ANSWER D

16. A CITATION FOR DRIVING 16 MPH OR MORE OVER THE LAWFUL SPEED LIMIT PUTS _____ POINTS ON YOUR LICENSE.
   A. 2
   B. 3
   C. 4
   D. 5

ANSWER C

17. IN WHICH OF THE FOLLOWING CASES IS AN INTERMEDIATE LICENSED DRIVER NOT PERMITTED TO DRIVE?
   A. He or she is age 16 and the time is 11:15 p.m.
   B. A licensed driver age 23 is in the front passenger seat.
   C. He or she is driving to work.
   D. He or she is age 17 and the time is 12:45 a.m.

ANSWER A

18. HEROIN AND COCAINE DON'T AFFECT YOUR PHYSICAL COORDINATION IN EXACTLY THE SAME WAYS AS ALCOHOL, _____.
   A. so they are less dangerous when driving
   B. but you will still be unable to drive safely
   C. and cocaine actually improves coordination
   D. but dextromethorphan does

ANSWER B

19. WHICH OF THE FOLLOWING BEST DESCRIBES WHO MUST ACCOMPANY THE LEARNER FOR LEGAL USE OF A LEARNERS LICENSE?
    E. A person with at least an Intermediate license
    F. A family member
    G. A licensed driver at least 21 years old in the front passenger seat
    H. A licensed driver at least 21 years old in any seat

ANSWER C

20. EFFECTS OF CHRONIC _____ USE INCLUDE EMPHYSEMA, HEART DISEASE, STROKE, IMPOTENCE, INFERTILITY, STRESS, AND CANCER OF NUMEROUS ORGANS.
    E. tobacco
    F. heroin
    G. cocaine
    H. alcohol

ANSWER A

21. WHICH OF THE FOLLOWING IS NOT A REASON THAT YOUNG PEOPLE ARE ESPECIALLY LIKELY TO ABUSE ALCOHOL AND DRUGS?
    A. Their organs are more vulnerable to alcohol
    B. They have more opportunities to consume alcohol
    C. They haven't developed healthier ways to cope
    D. They don't know how their bodies will react when they drink

ANSWER B

22. HARMFUL EFFECTS OF PAIN RELIEVERS INCLUDE
   _____.
   A. excessive buildup of stomach lining
   B. liver damage and thickening of the blood
   C. liver damage, thinning of the blood, and over-sensitivity to light
   D. None of the above

ANSWER C

23. YOU MAY OBTAIN AN INTERMEDIATE LICENSE IF YOU HAVE HELD A LEARNERS LICENSE FOR SIX MONTHS WITHOUT RECEIVING ANY TRAFFIC CONVICTIONS.
   A. TRUE
   B. FALSE

ANSWER A

24. _____ IS THE ACT OF DECLARING A DRIVERS LICENSE VOID AND TERMINATED WHEN IT IS DETERMINED THAT THE LICENSE WAS ISSUED THROUGH ERROR OR FRAUD.
   A. Revocation
   B. Suspension
   C. Cancellation
   D. Restriction

ANSWER C

25. _____ IS OFTEN THE FIRST DRUG MANY PEOPLE ABUSE.
   A. Cocaine
   B. Dextromethorphan
   C. Vicodin
   D. Alcohol

ANSWER D

26. ALCOHOLIC CARDIOMYOPATHY IS ESPECIALLY DANGEROUS BECAUSE _____.
   A. blood can leak from the heart into the chest cavity
   B. it can be passed to infants through the parents' genes
   C. sufferers sometimes show no symptoms until a fatal heart attack
   D. All of the above

ANSWER C

27. ACCORDING TO THE FINANCIAL RESPONSIBILITY LAW, IF YOU ARE THE OWNER OR OPERATOR OF A VEHICLE AND YOU ARE AT FAULT IN A COLLISION, YOU MAY BE REQUIRED TO _____ BEFORE YOUR DRIVING PRIVILEGE IS RESTORED.
   A. pay for the damages
   B. pass a driving test
   C. pay a fine
   D. take a traffic school course

ANSWER A

28. IN 2007, THE TWO MOST COSTLY COMPONENTS OF UNDERAGE DRINKING IN VIRGINIA WERE _____.
   A. violent crime and drug toxicity deaths
   B. violent crime and traffic collisions
   C. drug toxicity deaths and rehabilitation
   D. None of the above

ANSWER B

29. HOW MUCH ALCOHOL CAN YOU CONSUME AND STILL EXPECT TO BE ABLE TO DRIVE SAFELY?
   A. None
   B. Half a drink
   C. One drink
   D. Two drinks

ANSWER A

30. _____ SEPARATING LANES MEANS THAT CHANGING LANES IS HIGHLY DISCOURAGED FOR SAFETY REASONS.
   A. Reflective markers
   B. One solid white line
   C. One broken yellow line
   D. One broken white line

ANSWER B

31. A CURB OF THIS COLOR MEANS YOU MAY NOT STOP.
   A. Yellow
   B. Green
   C. Red

D. Blue

ANSWER C

32. WHICH OF THE FOLLOWING IS RECOMMENDED AS A WAY TO PREVENT VEHICLE BACKOVER DEATHS?
    A. Do not allow children to play in driveways
    B. Roll down your windows
    C. Look behind you the entire time you're backing up
    D. All of the above

ANSWER D

33. THE SHORT-TERM EFFECTS OF MARIJUANA INCLUDE _____.
    A. loss of coordination
    B. sleepiness
    C. increased heart rate
    D. All of the above

ANSWER D

34. WHICH OF THE FOLLOWING TYPES OF EMOTIONAL DISTRESS IS NOT DANGEROUS WHILE DRIVING?
    A. Anger
    B. Sadness
    C. Impatience
    D. None of the above

ANSWER D

35. YOU ARE NOT GUILTY OF DUI IF YOU ARE DRIVING IN AN UNSAFE MANNER AFTER DRINKING TOO MUCH COFFEE.
    A. TRUE
    B. FALSE

ANSWER B

36. IF YOU ARE DRIVING WHILE IMPAIRED, COMMIT MANSLAUGHTER OR VEHICULAR HOMICIDE, AND LEAVE THE SCENE OF THE CRIME, YOU WILL BE _____.
    A. fined up to $1,000 and imprisoned for up to 5 years
    B. fined up to $5,000 and imprisoned for up to 10 years
    C. fined up to $10,000 and imprisoned for up to 15 years
    D. fined up to $10,000 and imprisoned for up to 30 years

ANSWER D

37. YOU SHOULD HAVE YOUR BATTERY AND CHARGING SYSTEM CHECKED _____.
    A. at least once a year
    B. no more than once a year
    C. at least twice a year
    D. no more than twice a year

ANSWER A

38. IN 2009, ROUGHLY _____ OF HEAVY DRINKERS AGE 12 OR OLDER WERE CURRENT USERS OF ILLEGAL DRUGS.
    A. 13%

B. 20%
C. 33%
D. 50%

ANSWER C

39. WHICH OF THE FOLLOWING IS A CONSEQUENCE OF CHRONIC ALCOHOL USE?
    A. Gastritis
    B. Stomach ulcers
    C. Heartburn
    D. All of the above

ANSWER D

40. _____ ARE AN INDICATION THAT YOUR VEHICLE MAY BE DEVELOPING A COOLING SYSTEM PROBLEM.
    A. Abrupt changes or trends in engine temperature
    B. Foggy windows
    C. Squeaking brakes
    D. Low temperatures in the cabin

ANSWER A

ROAD SIGN QUESTIONS

70 QUESTIONS WITH ANSWERS AND EXPLANATIONS

1. This sign means?

    A. A flagger is stationed ahead to control road users.
    B. End of road construction.
    C. Road construction detour to the left.
    D. Road construction detour to the right.
    Answer A

2. This sign means?

    A. General service sign for a hospital.
    B. General service sign for a doctor's office.
    C. General service sign for a pharmacy.
    D. General service sign for parking.

Answer C

3. This warning sign means?

   A. Merging traffic entering from the left.
   B. Merging traffic entering from the right.
   C. Two lane traffic ahead.
   D. Intersection warning ahead.

   Answer A

4. What does this sign mean?

   A. A truck is 500 feet ahead of you.
   B. Slow down for the truck ahead.
   C. A farm vehicle, or tractor, is 500 feet ahead of you.
   D. Caution and keep a 500 foot distance between yourself and the farm vehicle ahead of you.

   Answer D

5. This sign means?

A. No parking anytime.

B. <u>Disabled</u> parking spot.

C. No parking here to the corner.

D. No stopping or standing.

Answer B

6. This sign means?

A. Divided highway ends.

B. Wrong way, turn around.

C. Traffic flows only in the direction of the arrow.

D. Divided highway begins.

Answer C

7. This sign means?

A. Divided highway ends. دُولہائی ختم ہو رہی ہے۔

B. Keep to the right of obstruction. رکاوٹ کے دائیں جانب سے گزریں۔

C. Keep to the left of obstruction. رکاوٹ کے بائیں جانب سے گزریں۔

D. Left lane ends. بائیں طرف والی لین ختم ہو رہی ہے۔

Answer B

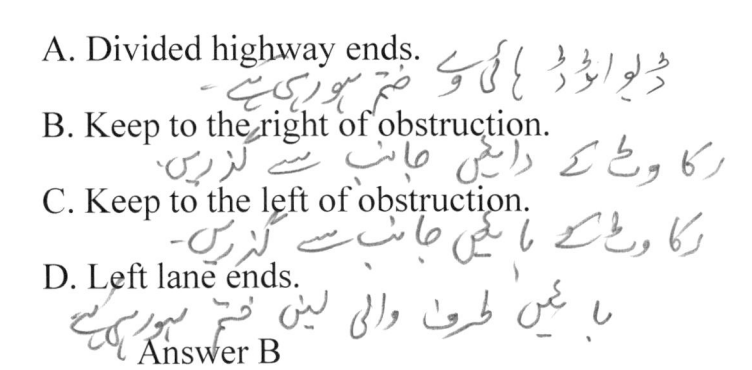

8. This sign means?

    A. Highway exit only.

    B. One lane traffic, keep to the right.

    C. Traffic is prohibited from entering a restricted roadway.

    D. Road closed, construction ahead.

    Answer C

9. This sign means?

    A. Right curve warning ahead.

    B. Merging traffic entering from the left.

C. Merging traffic entering from the right.

D. 2 Lane traffic ahead.

Answer C

10. This sign means?

A. Pedestrians only, no vehicle traffic.

B. School advance warning, you are entering a school zone.

C. Pedestrian crossing ahead.

D. Pedestrians ahead warning sign.

Answer B

11. This warning sign means?

A. Road ramp ahead.

B. Low clearance ahead.

C. Road narrows ahead.

D. Road under water ahead.

Answer B

12. This sign means?

A. Max speed 50 mph, minimum speed 30 mph in all conditions.

B. Speed limit is 50 mph, minimum fine of $50 for violations.

C. Max speed 50 mph, minimum speed 30 mph in ideal conditions.

D. Speed limit is 50 mph, minimum fine of $30 for violations.

Answer C

13. This warning sign means?

A. Winding road ahead, begins with a curve to the right.

B. The road curves to the left then to the right.

C. Winding road ahead, begins with a curve to the left.

D. Slippery when wet.

Answer A

14. This road sign means:

NO TURN ON RED

A. You may turn during the red light.

B. Pass only in the right lane.

C. One way street.

D. Do not turn during the red light.

Answer A

15. This sign means?

A. U-turn is prohibited.

B. No left lane.

C. Left lane ends.

D. No left turn.

Answer A

16. This sign means?

A. Two way traffic warning.

B. Warning for 2 lane highway.

C. Left lane ends ahead.

D. Right lane ends ahead.

Answer D

17. This sign means

A. Merging traffic is approaching from the right.

B. Winding road ahead.

C. Right lane ends ahead, stay to the left.

D. Divided highway ahead.

Answer C

18. This sign means?

A. No playing in the street.

B. No parking allowed.

C. No passing allowed.

D. No pedestrian traffic.

Answer B

19. This warning sign means?

A. U-turns allowed ahead.

B. Left curve ahead.

C. Circular intersection ahead.

D. Three-way intersection ahead.

Answer C

20. This warning sign means?

A. Road striping ahead.

B. Utility crew ahead.

C. Children's playground ahead.

D. Road maintenance crew ahead.

Answer C

21. This road sign means:

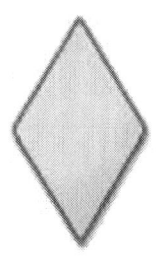

A. Warning of a hazard.

B. Yield right-of-way.

C. Railroad crossing.

D. Speed limit.

Answer A

22. This sign means?

A. Four-way intersection ahead.

B. Side road intersection ahead.

C. Intersection warning ahead, roadway ends, must turn right or left.

D. Y intersection ahead.

Answer C

23. This sign means?

A. Warning that a stop sign is ahead.

B. Forward traffic is not allowed.

C. Wrong way, do not enter.

D. A warning to stop right away.

Answer A

24. This sign means?

A. A sharp left curve warning.

B. A sharp right curve or turn.

C. V intersection ahead.

D. 2 Lane traffic ahead.

Answer B

25. This warning sign means?

A. Pavement ends ahead.

B. Lane ends ahead.

C. Road construction ahead.

D. Road closed ahead.

Answer A

26. This sign means?

A. Warning of a winding road ahead.

B. Warning of a right curve ahead.

C. Warning of merging traffic to the right.

D. Warning of a right turn ahead.

Answer B

27. If you see orange construction signs and cones on a freeway, you must:

    A. Slow down because the lane ends ahead.

    B. Be prepared for workers and equipment ahead.

    C. Change lanes and maintain your current speed.

    Answer B

28. This sign means

    A. All traffic turn left.

    B. No left turn.

    C. No U-turn.

    D. Truck route to the left.

    Answer B

29. This sign means

    A. Don't drink if you are going to drive.

    B. Slippery when wet.

    C. Road curves ahead.

D. You are approaching a hill.

Answer B

30. This warning sign means?

A. Pavement ends ahead.

B. Ahead is a sharp depression in the profile of the road.

C. Ahead is a narrow bridge warning.

D. Ahead is a sharp rise in the profile of the road.

Answer B

31. This road sign means:

A. Church.

B. First aid station.

C. Four-way intersection.

D. Railroad crossing.

Answer C

Answer D

32. This sign means?

A. Warning of divided highway ends ahead.

B. Warning of divided highway begins ahead.

C. Two way traffic advance warning.

D. Winding road advance warning.

Answer B

33. This sign means?

A. No hunting allowed.

B. Wildlife reserve area.

C. Deer crossing ahead.

D. State park area.

Answer C

34. This sign means?

   A. No u-turn.

   B. No right turn.

   C. No turn on red.

   D. No left turn.

   Answer B

35. Two sets of solid, double, yellow lines that are two or more feet apart:

   A. May be crossed to enter or exit a private driveway.

   B. May not be crossed for any reason.

   C. Should be treated as a separate traffic lane.

   Answer B

36. This sign means?

   A. Traffic flows only to the right.

   B. Traffic flows only to the left.

C. Your lane will end ahead.

D. Do not drive past this sign, turn around.

Answer D

37. What type of sign is this?

A. U. S. route sign.

B. County route sign.

C. State route sign.

D. Interstate route sign.

Answer C

38. This sign means?

A. Completely stop at sign and yield right-of-way traffic.

B. Slow down for an approaching intersection.

C. Slow down, completely stop if required, yield right-of-way traffic.

D. Wrong way, do not enter.

Answer C

39. This sign means?

A. Church crossing.

B. Pedestrian crossing.

C. Pedestrian traffic only.

D. School crossing.

Answer D

40. This warning sign means?

A. Left curve ahead warning.

B. Merging traffic from the right.

C. Hairpin curve ahead, extreme right curve.

D. Right turn ahead warning.

Answer C

41. This warning sign means?

A. Right lane stays to the right, left lane stays to the left.

B. Keep to the right, merging traffic ahead.

C. Keep to the left, merging traffic ahead.

D. Traffic is permitted to pass on either side of an island or obstruction.

ANSWER D

42. This sign means?

A. Highway exit only.

B. One lane traffic, keep to the right.

C. Traffic is prohibited from entering a restricted roadway.

D. Road closed, construction ahead.

Answer C

43. This road sign means:

A. No U-turn.

B. Curve.

C. Turn right or left.

D. Traffic flows only in the direction of the arrow.

    Answer D

44. This sign means

A. Divided highway ahead.

B. One-way traffic ahead.

C. Four-lane highway ahead.

D. Divided highway ends.

    Answer D

45. This warning sign means?

A. Right lane stays to the right, left lane stays to the left.

B. Keep to the right, merging traffic ahead.

C. Keep to the left, merging traffic ahead.

D. Traffic is permitted to pass on either side of an island or obstruction.

Answer D

46. What type of sign is this?

A. State route sign.

B. U. S. route sign.

C. County route sign.

D. Interstate route sign.

Answer B

47. This sign means?

A. General information sign for a library.

B. General information sign for a bus stop.

C. General information sign for a school.

D. General information sign for a park.

Answer A

48. This sign means?

A. No motor vehicles allowed.

B. No pedestrian crossing.

C. Pedestrian crossing.

D. School crossing.

Answer D

49. This warning sign means?

A. Winding road ahead.

B. The road ahead curves sharply right, then left.

C. The road ahead turns sharply left.

D. The road ahead curves sharply left, then right.

Answer B

50. This sign means

A. Slow down if an emergency vehicle is approaching.

B. Look both ways as you cross the intersection.

C. Always come to a full stop at the intersection.

D. Slow down and be prepared to stop if necessary.

Answer D

51. This sign means?

A. No left turn.

B. No u-turn.

C. No right turn.

D. No turn on red.

Answer A

52. This sign means?

A. Merging traffic from the right.

B. Winding road, use caution.

C. Slippery when wet, use caution.

D. Sharp left curve then right curve, use caution.

Answer C

53. This sign means?

A. Route H highway sign.

B. General service sign for a highway.

C. General service sign for a hotel.

D. General service sign for a hospital.

Answer D

54. This sign means

A. Trucks under 18,000 lbs. allowed.

B. Hill ahead.

C. Truck stop ahead.

D. No trucks allowed

Answer B

55. This warning sign means?

A. This road or street terminates ahead.

B. Do not enter, wrong way.

C. Two-way traffic ends ahead.

D. Wrong way, turn around.

Answer A

56. This sign means?

A. Come to a complete stop, proceed only when safe to do so.

B. Slow down and yield to oncoming traffic

C. Stop only to avoid an accident

D. Slow down and proceed if traffic allows.

Answer A

57. What type of sign is this?

A. Interstate route sign.

B. County route sign.

C. State route sign.

D. U. S. route sign.

Answer A

58. This warning sign means.

A. Reverse curve ahead.

B. One-way traffic ahead.

C. A divided highway ends ahead.

D. A divided highway begins ahead.

Answer C

59. What type of sign is this?

A. State route sign.

B. U. S. route sign.

C. County route sign.

D. Interstate route sign.

Answer C

60. This sign means?

A. Warning sign for truck ramp.

B. Warning sign for draw bridge ahead.

C. Warning sign for hill ahead.

D. No trucks warning sign.

Answer C

61. This sign means?

A. General information sign for an aircraft manufacturing plant.

B. No fly zone ahead.

C. General information sign for an airport.

D. Low flying aircraft warning.

Answer C

62. The correct hand signal for stopping is:

A. Right hand and arm pointing downward.

B. Left hand and arm pointing straight out.

C. Left hand and arm pointing downward.

D. Left hand and arm pointing upward.

Answer C

63. This sign means?

A. T-Road intersection ahead.

B. A two-way intersection ahead.

C. A four-way intersection ahead.

D. Side road intersection ahead.

Answer C

64. This sign means?

A. Narrow bridge warning.

B. Merging traffic from the right.

C. Left lane ends ahead.

D. Soft shoulder warning.

Answer A

65. This road sign means:

A. Right lane ends soon, merge left.

B. Soft shoulders.

C. Low place in the road.

D. Lane ends soon, merge right

Answer A

66. This sign means

A. Continue at your current speed.

B. You must stop ahead.

C. Speeding is not allowed.

D. There is a traffic signal ahead.

Answer D

67. This sign means?

A. Maximum legal speed is 50 mph in ideal conditions.

B. Maximum legal speed is 50 mph in all weather conditions.

C. Minimum legal speed is 50 mph in ideal conditions.

D. Minimum legal speed is 50 mph in all weather conditions.

Answer A

68. This sign means

A. One-way traffic

B. Intersection ahead.

C. Merging traffic from the right.

D. Highway curves ahead.

Answer C

69. This sign means?

A. Advance warning of a low speed sharp left curve.

B. Road curves right, then turns left.

C. Advance warning of a winding road.

D. Advance warning of a right curve.

Answer A

70. A white painted curb means:

A. Loading zone for freight or passengers.

B. Loading zone for passengers or mail only.

C. Loading zone for freight only.

Answer B

DEFENSIVE DRIVING

50 QUESTIONS WITH EXPLANATORY ANSWERS

1. When traveling behind a motorcycle:

    A. Allow a following distance of at least 2 car lengths

    B. Allow at least 2 seconds of following distance

    C. Allow at least 4 seconds of following distance

    D. Allow a following distance of at least 4 motorcycle lengths

    Answer C

2. If you are following a truck that swings left before making a right turn at an intersection, you should remember that it is very dangerous to:

    A. Try to squeeze between the truck and curb to make a right turn

    B. Apply your brakes until the truck has completed the turn

    C. Violate the 4-second following distance rule

    D. Honk your horn at the truck driver

    Answer A

3. Preparing to smoke and smoking while driving:

> A. Do not affect driving abilities
>
> B. Help maintain driver alertness
>
> C. Are distracting activities
>
> D. Are not distracting activities
>
> Answer C

4. The most important thing to remember about speed management and curves is to:

    > A. Drive at the posted speed limit as you enter the curve, then slow down at the sharpest part of the curve
    >
    > B. Slow down before you enter the curve
    >
    > C. Accelerate gently before you enter the curve
    >
    > D. Drive at the posted speed limit of the roadway, before, throughout, and after the curve
    >
    > Answer C

5. If you want to get off from a freeway, but you missed your exit, you should:

    > A. Go to the next exit, and get off the freeway there
    >
    > B. Make a U-turn through the median
    >
    > C. Pull onto the shoulder and back your car to the exit

  D. Flag down a police officer for an escort back to your exit

  Answer A

6. When no signs, signals, or police tell you what to do at an intersection, the law states that:

  A. Drivers on the right must yield to drivers on the left

  B. There are no laws stating who must yield

  C. Drivers going straight must yield to drivers turning left at the intersection

  D. Drivers turning left must yield to drivers going straight through the intersection

  Answer D

7. Highway hypnosis is a driver condition that can result from:

  A. Staring at the roadway for long periods of time

  B. Frequent rest stops

  C. Too much sleep the night before your trip

  D. Short trips on expressways

  Answer A

8. To avoid last minute moves, you should be looking down the road to where your vehicle will be in about ____.

  A. 5 to 10 seconds

B. 10 to 15 seconds

C. 15 to 20 seconds

Answer B

9. If you stop at a railroad crossing with more than one track:

    A. Wait until you have a clear view of all tracks

    B. Stop on the railroad track and watch for another train

    C. Go through as soon as the train passes

    D. Go through when one of the tracks is free

    Answer A

10. You are waiting to turn left at a multilane intersection, and opposing traffic is blocking your view, you should:

    A. Accelerate rapidly when the first lane you need to cross is clear

    B. Wait until you can see all the lanes you need to cross before going ahead with your turn

    C. Wait for the opposing driver to wave you across the intersection

    D. Edge your car into each lane of opposing traffic as soon as it clears

    Answer B

11. When sharing the road with a truck, it is important to remember that, in general, trucks:

    A. Take longer distances than cars to stop

    B. Require less time to pass on a downgrade than cars

    C. Require less turning radius than cars

    D. Require less time to pass on an incline than cars

    Answer A

12. When entering a freeway:

    A. Vehicles on the freeway must always yield the right-of-way to vehicles that are entering the freeway.

    B. You must yield the right-of-way to vehicles already on the freeway.

    C. Increase your speed even if the way is not clear.

    D. You must always drive at the same speed as the rest of the traffic.

    Answer B

13. When driving on a freeway entrance ramp, you should look for a gap in freeway traffic by:

    A. Looking in the inside rearview mirror only

    B. Looking in the sideview mirror only

    C. Looking in both rearview and sideview mirrors

D. Looking in your mirrors and turning your head to look over your shoulder

Answer D

14. You need to use extra caution when driving near a pedestrian using a white cane because:

    A. He or she is deaf

    B. He or she has a mental disability

    C. He or she is blind

    D. He or she has a walking problem

    Answer C

15. On two-lane, two-way streets or highways, you should start left turns:

    A. Close to the center line

    B. Close to the outside line

    C. In the center of the lane

    D. Anywhere in the lane

    Answer A

16. teenage drivers are more likely to be involved in a crash when:

    A. They are driving with their pet as a passenger

    B. They are driving with adult passengers

    C. They are driving with teenage passengers

D. They are driving without any passengers

Answer C

17. If you are driving behind a motorcycle, you must:

A. Allow the motorcycle to use a complete lane

B. Drive on the shoulder beside the motorcycle

C. Allow the motorcycle to use only half a lane

D. Pass in the same lane where the motorcycle is driving

Answer A

18. After a train has passed, you should:

A. Check again for approaching trains and proceed with caution

B. Wait for a green light

C. Proceed across the tracks

D. Blow horn and proceed

Answer A

19. A safe speed to drive your car

A. Is the posted speed limit.

B. Is less than the posted speed limit.

C. Depends on the weather and road conditions.

D. Depends on the mechanical skill of the driver.

Answer C

20. When driving near a blind pedestrian who is carrying a white cane or using a guide dog, you should:

  A. Slow down and be prepared to stop

  B. Take the right-of-way

  C. Proceed normally

  D. Drive away quickly

  Answer A

21. Minimum speed signs are designed to

  A. Keep traffic flowing smoothly.

  B. Show current local road conditions.

  C. Test future traffic signal needs.

  D. Assure pedestrian safety.

  Answer A

22. When passing a bicyclist, you should:

  A. Blast your horn to alert the bicyclist

  B. Move as far left as possible

  C. Remain in the center of the lane

D. Put on your four-way flashers

Answer B

23. Who must yield when a driver is turning and a pedestrian is crossing without a traffic light?

A. Whoever started last

B. The driver

C. Whoever is slower

D. The pedestrian

Answer B

24. To turn left on multi-lane streets and highways, you should start from:

A. The middle of the intersection

B. The right lane

C. The left lane

D. Any lane

Answer C

25. Always use your seat belt:

A. Unless the vehicle was built before 1978.

B. Unless you are in a limousine.

C. When the vehicle is equipped with seat belt

Answer C

26. You drive defensively when you:

   A. Always put one car length between you and the car ahead.

   B. Look only at the car in front of you while driving.

   C. Keep your eyes moving to look for possible hazards.

   Answer C

27. It is best to keep a space cushion:

   A. Only in back of your vehicle

   B. Only on the left and right side of your vehicle

   C. Only in front of the vehicle

   D. On all sides of the vehicle

   Answer D

28. Which of the following statements about blind spots is true?

   A. They are eliminated if you have one outside mirror on each side of the vehicle.

   B. Large trucks have bigger blind spots than most passenger vehicles.

   C. Blind spots can be checked by looking in your rear view mirrors.

Answer B

29. When entering a highway from an entrance ramp, you should generally:

>A. Enter above the speed of traffic to get ahead

>B. Enter slowly to avoid other vehicles

>C. Stop first, then slowly enter traffic

>D. Accelerate to the speed of traffic

>Answer D

30. Allowing a space cushion is important because it:

>A. Prevents distractions from other vehicles

>B. Allows you time to react to situations

>C. Keeps traffic flowing at a safe pace

>D. Keeps other drivers alert

>Answer B

31. One of the rules of defensive driving is

>A. Look straight ahead as you drive.

>B. Stay alert and keep your eyes moving.

>C. Expect that other drivers will make up for your errors.

>D. Be confident that you can avoid danger at the last minute.

Answer B

32. At night, it is hardest to see:

    A. Road signs

    B. Pedestrians

    C. Other motorists

    D. Street lights

    Answer B

33. The four-second rule refers to how one should:

    A. Yield to other cars

    B. Turn at stop signs

    C. Follow another car

    D. Cross an intersection

    Answer C

34. U-turns in residential districts are legal:

    A. On a one-way street on a green arrow.

    B. When there are no vehicles approaching nearby.

    C. Across two sets of solid double, yellow lines.

    Answer B

35. The only time you do not have to stop for a school bus whose red lights are flashing and stop arm is extended is when you:

A. Are driving on the opposite side of a divided highway

B. Are behind the bus

C. See no children present

D. Can safely pass on the left

Answer A

36. The law gives _____ the right of way at intersections.

A. No one

B. Drivers turning left

C. Drivers going straight

D. Drivers turning right

Answer A

37. Seat belts can be most effective as injury preventive devices when they are worn by

A. The person driving the car.

B. Passengers when they are on a long drive.

C. All occupants of a car being driven on an expressway.

D. Passengers and the driver whenever they are in the car.

Answer D

38. When exiting a highway, you should slow down:

A. On the main road, just before the exit lane

B. Once you see the toll booth

C. Once you have moved into the exit lane

D. When you first see the exit sign

Answer C

39. You can park and leave your car

A. In a tunnel.

B. 30 feet from a railroad crossing.

C. Between a safety zone and the curb.

D. None of the above.

Answer D

40. When a school bus has its lights flashing and its stop arm extended, you must:

A. Stop at least 10 feet away from the bus

B. Pass if children have exited the bus

C. Stop if the bus is on the opposite side of a barrier

D. Drive slowly by the bus

Answer A

41. Drivers who eat and drink while driving:

A. Have no driving errors

B. Have trouble driving slow

C. Are better drivers because they are not hungry

D. Have trouble controlling their vehicles

Answer D

42. When passing on a multi-lane highway:

A. Be sure the passing lane is clear

B. Pass only on the right

C. Watch for oncoming traffic

D. There is no need to signal

Answer A

43. To make a right turn at the corner, you:

A. May not enter the bicycle lane.

B. Should only merge into the bicycle lane if you stop before turning.

C. Must merge into the bicycle lane before turning.

Answer C

44. Drivers entering a roundabout or traffic circle:

A. Must stop before entering

B. Must yield to drivers in the roundabout or traffic circle

C. Have the right of way if they arrive first

D. Have the right of way if there are two lanes

Answer B

45. Under normal conditions, a safe following distance between your car and the car ahead is:

A. Fifty feet.

B. One car length.

C. Three second behind the vehicle you follow

D. One hundred feet

Answer C

46. When you are merging onto the freeway, you should be driving:

A. At or near the same speed as the traffic on the freeway.

B. 5 to 10 MPH slower than the traffic on the freeway.

C. The posted speed limit for traffic on the freeway.

Answer A

47. Collisions can happen more often when:

A. All vehicles are traveling about the same speed.

B. One lane of traffic is traveling faster than the other lanes.

C. One vehicle is traveling faster or slower than the flow of traffic.

Answer C

48. On long trips you can prevent drowsiness by

A. Turning on your car radio.

B. Slowing down so you can react better.

C. Stopping at regular intervals for a rest.

D. Moving your eyes from side to side as you drive.

Answer C

49. To pass a slower-moving vehicle on a two-lane road you must:

A. Not cross the center line

B. Flash your lights to oncoming traffic

C. Use the shoulder

D. Use that lane that belongs to oncoming traffic

Answer D

50. When you drive through an area where children are playing, you should expect them:

    A. To know when it is safe to cross

    B. To stop at the curb before crossing the street

    C. To run out in front of you without looking

    D. Not to cross unless they are with an adult

    Answer C

ABOUT THE 2018 STUDY GUIDE

This practical test manual is surely a jinx breaker when it comes to passing your Virginia DMV permit license test. Using this practice test guide alongside the Virginia driving manual is all you need to ace the DMV permit test. Our over 300 multiple choice questions were prepared right out of the manual to give you the edge as you prepare.

While studying the questions, you will be able to see the correct answer alongside a detailed explanation as to how the answer came about. This would help you not just to know the correct answer, but to understand the reason behind the answer. As you continue to practice with this manual, you become totally knowledgeable and will improve over time. It is advisable you read the Virginia driver's license manual before you write the exam. This will enable you get acquainted with all the questions and answers. I hope you enjoy the tests.

This book is split into five categories;

- General Questions
- Road Sign Questions
- Drugs and Alcohol Questions
- Traffic Sign Questions
- Defensive driving Questions.

To achieve a successful test, I would advise you to repeat all the questions till you consistently achieve a minimum score of 85%. Achieving this will help you score much higher when you write the original test.

This practical test has over 300 test question and it is a perfect way to prepare for the actual test. The questions contained here are similar to the actual test questions. Using this practical preparation method as opposed to the time-consuming DMV driver's handbook, you will learn the basic driving skills, road signs, traffic signs, and all about drugs, alcohol and driving. This book will also teach you how to answer the trick questions which always appears on the test.

How to pass the DMV Permit Test on First Try

The learner's permit test can be actually difficult for first-time test takers. It is reported that about 70% fail the test the first time, and probably need to try once again. It is probably frustrating to take the test more than once since you'd have to face the queue again or probably pay another fee which you might not have.

It is now obvious that the best way to pass the test is to pass it the first time and move on without any hassle. It is actually not difficult to pass; you only need to know the secrets of passing the DMV test.

What are the secrets of passing the DMV permit test? I will show you right away;

- **Remember those Small Details**

You can engage the DMV manual to know more. It might seem inconsequential and difficult to remember, because they seem less important to driving safety. But you should understand the fact that no knowledge is a waste when it comes to driving and slamming home your DMV permit test.

- **Attend a driver's education class before taking the main permit test**

If the test taker is still in high school, the driver's education class usually ends with the official DMV permit test. The DMV offers some sort of driver's education classes for intending test takers. This learning process is imperative if you intend to pass your permit test at first try.

- **Consult experienced drivers for more explanations**

When you come across experienced drivers who are driving, you can ask questions. This would help you understand the driving process better.

- **Understanding the rules makes it easier to recall**

Most of us might be tempted to cram the road rules questions, but they are quite abstract and difficult to remember. Knowing how to apply it practically might make its remembrance natural for you.

- **Remember to answer all questions**

Any unanswered question is considered a wrong question. It wouldn't hurt making a simple guess on questions you have no clue about. So be sure to fill in answers to all questions.

- **Use common sense and do not overemphasize or think about each question**

- Always answer or solve the easy questions first, and go back to the unanswered or hard questions letter.

- Prepare in advance by practicing and reading all available resources that would help you pass the test.

- Skip any question you have no idea about. Time is crucial when it comes to passing the DMV test.

New 2018 Driving Laws

Effective January 1, 2018

Marijuana Use In Vehicles

It is illegal to smoke or ingest marijuana or any marijuana product while driving a motor vehicle upon a highway or while riding as a passenger in a motor vehicle being driven upon a highway..

Buses and Seatbelts

Effective July 1, 2018, it is required that a passenger in a bus equipped with seat belts to be properly restrained by a safety belt, except as specified.

New DMV

Effective April 2018, an online identification and application process will now be offered by the DMV. All applicants will now be given the opportunity to start their electronic application before they visit the DMV. You are expected to bring an application confirmation alongside while coming to the office.

Made in the USA
Middletown, DE
21 November 2018